Contents

Welcome to Germany

'My name is Moritz. I'm here with my family and my dog Paula in our garden.' Moritz.

Moritz Parisius is nine years old. He lives with his mum, dad and older sister Lisa. They have a dog called Paula and a cat called Söcke. The family lives in a village called Bergshausen, in the middle of Germany. You can see where it is on the map on page 5.

▲ *From left to right:*
Moritz's dad
Moritz
Moritz's mum
Lisa, (Moritz's sister)

► *Germany's place in the world.*

▼ *Germany is a large country, right in the middle of Europe.*

GERMANY

Capital city:	Berlin
Land area:	357,000 square kilometres
Population:	82 million people
Main language:	German
Main religions:	Roman Catholic (in the south) and Protestant (in the north)

The Land and Weather

Germany is right in the middle of Europe. The north of Germany is bordered by the sea, and the land is flat. There are lots of hills in the centre of Germany and in the south there are high mountains.

Around Bergshausen the land is quite hilly. There are fields and woods outside the village.

▲ *A sunny day in the village of Bergshausen.*

▶ *There are some beautiful rivers in southern Germany.*

'It's fun living in a village. There are lots of places to play.' Moritz.

◀ *During the summer, many Germans go to the beaches in the north.*

The weather in Germany changes from one time of the year to another. Summer is usually warm and sunny. Winter is much colder. There is ice and snow, especially in the high mountains in the south of Germany.

▼ *Moritz and Lisa go for a bicycle ride in the autumn rain.*

8

Just a few kilometres away from Bergshausen lies the town of Kassel. Most Germans live in large cities or towns, such as Kassel.

▲ *There are many shops and offices in Kassel's busy town centre.*

At Home

In Germany many people rent their homes. In towns and cities most people live in flats instead of houses. The people who live in flats don't have gardens, but some have balconies.

▲ *Each flat has a doorbell and letterbox by the main entrance.*

▶ *In busy towns flats jostle for space with tall office blocks.*

'We come to
our local park
when we want to
play outside.'
Sonja (right).

11

▶ *These old houses in Bergshausen have wooden frames.*

▼ *Moritz, Lisa and Paula the dog enjoy watching television in their lounge.*

The Parisius family lives in a modern house. Mr and Mrs Parisius do not want their home to harm the environment. They try not to use too much gas and electricity.

Like many German families, the Parisius family can afford expensive goods, such as a car, a television and a computer.

▼ *Sometimes Moritz finds some interesting creatures in the garden.*

13

German Food

Germans enjoy their food, and they are proud of their country's special dishes.

German people buy a lot of their food in supermarkets, but there are still many small shops too. Most neighbourhoods have their own baker and butcher.

▲ Favourite evening snacks are sausages, dark bread called pumpernickel, and pickled fish called rollmops.

▶ Colourful outdoor markets sell fresh fruit and vegetables.

◀ Customers choose their own vegetables at the supermarket.

15

▲ *The Parisius family sits down to a tasty traditional breakfast.*

The Parisius family often have a large breakfast, with boiled eggs, bread and cheese. There is sometimes ham or meat paste too.

Many Germans like to have a cooked meal at lunch time. In towns and cities, hungry office workers crowd into cafés or busy restaurants.

▶ *On warm days, you can have lunch at an outdoor café.*

'People come to my stall for a tasty snack of sausage and bread.'
Mr Graf, food stall owner.

17

At Work

Industries making goods such as cars, electrical goods and machinery, provide a lot of jobs in Germany.

▼ *At the stock exchange in Frankfurt, people invest money in German industries.*

'I love to help people. Being a psychiatrist is my dream job.' Moritz's mum.

In Bergshausen, some people work at the farms in the village. Many others work at a large car factory nearby.

Moritz's mum works as a kind of doctor called a psychiatrist. On some days she works in a surgery that is part of the Parisius' home.

◀ *Mr Schmidtt is a pig farmer in Bergshausen.*

At School

German children begin school by going part-time to a nursery called a *kindergarten*. Primary school starts when they are six years old.

► *Children crowd on to a bus to be taken to school.*

▼ *These children are hard at work, building a model rocket.*

The school day begins at 8 o'clock in the morning. There are lessons all morning, with two short breaks. When lessons finish at 1 o'clock, the children go home in time for lunch.

▲ *Children work in pairs on the school computers.*

There are about 25 boys and girls in Moritz's class.

Moritz has just started at a new school. It is in the nearby town of Kassel and he travels there every day by bus.

Moritz's school is in a brand-new building. There is plenty of modern equipment, and each class has its own computers.

▼ *Every afternoon, Moritz has to do some homework.*

'I like art and English, but my favourite subject is football!' Moritz.

Free Time

Sports are very popular in Germany, especially football and swimming.

Bergshausen has its own youth club, run by a local church. Children go there to play games such as table tennis.

▲ *Lisa is learning to play the mandolin in her spare time.*

▶ *This girl is learning how to unicycle at a youth club.*

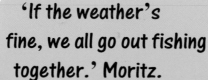

'If the weather's fine, we all go out fishing together.' Moritz.

24

25

Looking Ahead

Germany is a modern, wealthy country. Its factories make goods such as cars, mobile phones and hi-fi equipment which are sold all over the world.

Many Germans are worried about the harm that cars and industry can do to the environment. They want to stop pollution in towns and cities.

'When I grow up, I want to play football for Germany!' Moritz.

▶ *New buildings shoot up in a city centre.*

December Biscuits

Moritz and his family like to eat December biscuits on St Nicholas' Day (on 6 December) and at Christmas. They are very easy to make.

You will need:

100 g butter
75 g caster sugar
1 egg
200 g plain flour
half teaspoon mixed spice
half teaspoon ground cinammon
1–2 tablespoons of milk

- First, cream the butter and sugar together in a mixing bowl.

▲ *Moritz starts to make the dough.*

- Then, separate the egg yolk and beat it into the mixture. Sift in the flour and spices and mix well. Add the milk and knead the mixture into a soft dough.

- Roll out the mixture on a floured board, until it is about 5 mm thick. Cut out star or moon shapes. Brush the top of each shape with the egg white.

- Ask an adult to bake the biscuits for 10–12 minutes at Gas Mark 6/200 °C.

▲ *Moritz's mum and sister use oven gloves to take the biscuits out of the hot oven.*

Germany Fact File

Money Facts

◄ German money is the mark, which is divided into 100 pfennings. £1 is worth about 3 marks. Carl Friedrich Gauss, the famous mathematician, can be seen on the 10 mark note.

Famous People

Famous German people include Johann Guttenberg who invented the first-ever printing press, during the fifteenth century and the Brothers Grimm, who wrote Grimm's Fairy Tales. Former Wimbledon champions, Boris Becker and Steffi Graf are both from Germany.

River Facts

Germany has several major rivers, such as the Rhine, the Elbe and the Danube.

The German Flag

▼ The red, black and gold represent a long struggle for a united Germany.

Mountain Facts

The highest mountain is the Zugspitze, in the Alps. It is 2,963 metres high.

The Berlin Wall

After the Second World War, Germany was divided into East Germany and West Germany. In 1961, East Germany's government built a wall through Berlin to stop its people going to West Germany. In 1990 East Germany and West Germany became one country again and the Berlin Wall was torn down. ▼

Car Industry

Germany is famous for producing high quality cars, which are sold all over the world.

Delicatessen

There are many different types of sausage to choose from in Germany, from *bratwurst* to *salami*. ▼

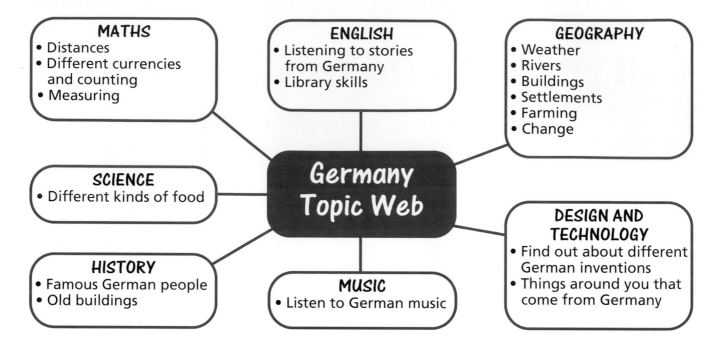

Extension Activities

Geography
- Do we eat any foods that come from Germany? Investigate packets and labels.
- What is the weather like in Germany? Look for clues in the photographs and text of this book.
- How many different kinds of building can children find in this book? What are the different buildings used for?
- Ask the children to try to work out which photographs in the book show different types of settlement.

Maths
- Make your own German money, with marks and pfennigs. Talk about what things you might buy if you went to Germany. You might even learn to count to ten in German.
- Look at some weather data, in numerical form, for German locations. Make graphs to show temperature and hours of sunshine.

English
- Most children will have encountered at least one or two German folk stories. Talk about the brothers Grimm.
- Bergshausen is quite close to the German town of Hamelin. Find it on a map and tell the story of the Pied Piper.

History
- Look at photographs in this book, and search for buildings and locations that are modern. Can the children find any examples of buildings or places that they think are old-fashioned?

DT
- Make the December biscuits.

Music
- Learn some German folk songs or carols: *O Christmas Tree* and *Silent Night*.

RE
- Investigate the German religious festivals of Shrovetide, St Martin's Day and St Nicholas' Day.
- How do German children celebrate the Christian festivals of Christmas and Easter?

Glossary

Balconies Special areas outside the windows of flats where people can sit, hang washing or grow plants.

Environment The surrounding area. It includes the land, air and water around where you live.

Invest To put money into businesses to make more money.

Mandolin An old-fashioned type of stringed instrument.

Pollution Anything that can harm the natural environment.

Psychiatrist A type of doctor who treats illnesses of the mind.

Rent To pay money to the owner of a home in order to live there.

Surgery A place where a doctor treats his or her patients.

Unicycle A cycle with only one wheel. Unicycles are very difficult to balance.

Further Information

Fiction:
Any of the Grimm's Fairy Tales.

Non-fiction:
A Family From Germany by Sonja Peters (Wayland, 1997)

A Flavour of Germany (Food and Festivals series) by Mike Hirst (Wayland, 1999)

Germany (Picture a Country) by Henry Pluckrose (Watts, 1998)

Useful Addresses:
Embassy of the Federal Republic of Germany, 34 Belgrave Square, London SW1 8QB provides information about Germany.

Goethe-Institut London, 50 Princes Gate, Exhibition Road, London SW7 2PH organizes exhibitions, films and information services. The Institute's libraries also lend tapes, books and video cassettes.

Index

All the numbers in **bold** refer to photographs.